T0244504

AN
ORANGE

TED DODSON
AN ORANGE

PUBLISHED BY
PIONEER WORKS PRESS
AND WONDER

ISBN 978-3-16-148410-O-O
FIRST EDITION ©2021

for MARIE

CONTENTS

AN ORANGE

It would be too easy to say love vanished from
    the earth, to say
an emptied mountain struck its hollowest note
    and sounded
unlike anything else. I text the same three
    people every day, sometimes
four. How fast that dream left me when I woke
    out of it, snorted up
into a catalog of faces fastened with long and
    draping hair. Unrecognizably,
I am thinking of something else. Not a dream or
    a short transparent reality
like the outer bend of my eyes or a limping
    memory poking around the calendar
for an approximate location. Something else.
    And I really don't feel I know enough
to say what it is. Shouldn't a work of sufficient
    emotion optimize any morning
into a cascade of murmuring strings that appear
    to fix the ground
to an object vast enough to be in the continual
    distance? I knocked on that door
once, and I think behind it was all spaghetti.
    Life's things do pile up,
though I'm daily assured I can be driven into a
    normative clarity,

wiping away thoughts like they'd accumulated
on a windshield.

Andrew sent me a new story of his yesterday
about an empty-handed search
for a fabled painting of Guibert, its sole
evidence of existence was an appearance
in *L'Homme au chapeau rouge*, which I have not
read. He later emailed me
to clarify the search was fictional and the
narrative cribbed from *L'Homme*.
The story is beautiful, one of my favorites of his
now. The image of never having
been though still having, distinct and existent
as anything else, a life,
hangs clear and unguarded and doubles as a
volume of forgetting one
pages through while sitting up from bed or
even walking to the kitchen
maybe for coffee if I remembered to buy a bag
of beans at the store yesterday.

[BROOKLYN, 5/25/18]

To have come this far

only to be reduced to dew

heroically is a fitting though limp

insurrection disguising what looked

to be a better plan. Once

I witnessed a clear vision

and was full envy. But who would feel

otherwise? The affect of lecture takes

art when no one is listening

and this is by necessity. Let's talk

materials. Being unrequired

to ratify decency as the central

non-combustible tenet of worldly affairs

courage filed alongside myth

and fiction. Within this index

some of us sit with

an invited guest who gifts

a parcel of land tattooed

in a far national

corner, a lip too remote

to ever reach, and this was by design.

I took off my clothes

so I could see my ass

see if the gym gave me any

classicism but without a mirror

I'm more or less intractable

in relation to my own body's

semiotics, trying to peer around

the corner of myself. I just hope

a man or a woman upon finding me

wiped naked across an unfamiliar

coast, having vanished

on an ill-fated vacation,

at least say what a waste

then repost and enshrine

my likeness as a minor

cultural reference point.

Could be too much

to ask. Instead, I interview

with the panopticon.

It sees me and all I see

is a generic avatar, a little ghost

or an octopus emoji. Do I

have any interest in wearing

a RompHim? The official future

outfit for stormtroopers, partying with

Corona Light and a sponsored

photoshoot? A bottle of rosé

floats in the pool, manufactured

for buoyancy. Solidarity is opted-in

for history and all I have to show for it

is this scam, me and everyone

I know. Do the drugs even work?

I'll say I've had enough of perspective,

but there are more empty rooms,

empty for the sake of their emptiness,

where I'd be content to wait around

for a phone to ding. I'll try that hat on

again under the protective guise

of a California saffron blaze,

safe from the rough quenching

of gathered foams and spume

lathered from chlorinated shores

appearing from the air as winsome

sapphire pits. I adjust my privacy settings

to include the walls of my apartment

with the curtains drawn, a gratifying effort

to collectivize as the eye

of Sauron whose power thirst

was a front for his voyeurism,

catching Frodo and Sam bareback

on the side of the Misty Mountains,

pretending he didn't see so he'd

never have to stop watching.

"Destroyed by my lust for hobbit ass"

would be a good title for Sauron's biopic

or maybe this poem, too. O'Hara wrote about

not having to leave the city to enjoy greenery,

also the pleasant cold of a hilltop

upstate and driving up the West Side Highway

presumably. I'm amazed how one's point of view translates

to desire depending on the direction of
  approach

or the speed of arrival or the voluntary
  retreat

of oneself to a solitary place even if it's just

the back seat of a sedan. Austerity measures

your propinquity to yourself, weighing

throwing us or ourselves over

the side of a bridge with a view

of the burning tide gratifying

our aerodynamic contours.

How heavenly we could be if only

we had a world where we were.

[TORONTO, 7/5/18]

At the center of what lives and dreams,
an unmistakable and debtless intelligence
or a cataclysm of unmanaged resources
that could buy time as if it were being sold,
a PowerBar or blank note pad. An unfinished
categorizing of OTC suggestions could work
my heart blue then yellow sky
over the long drool of attractions, their
copious marginalia. Awareness swells
under the surface like music fills a balloon.

There were two of us then there are several
invented by way of an elementary connection
spanning a room provided for too many
to wait in. To get back to basics would mean
valuing ourselves last or breaking a halo of reason.
That much was ever certain but hardly assured.

[WASHINGTON, D.C., 10/3/18]

I hate a guy with a car and no sense of humor.
—*Halloween* (DIR. JOHN CARPENTER, 1978)

Soph texts me a picture.

It's a parked car at the end

of her street. It's the exact

station wagon from *Halloween*

Michael Myers steals to escape

the asylum where he was

confined during the years after

he murdered his sister in a

psychosexual fit. My first car

was a 1993 Volkswagen. The

speedometer didn't work

which was funny as in

it made me nervous, induced

a fearfulness of the endless

or undetermined, probably a latent

cultural prerogative's structural

trigger. How fast am I going

and when will this be over?

It's easy to determine the horrific

motivations of monsters to violence.

They're often banal, clear

and resolved, a shape inexorably

approaching at a determined

velocity. A friend invited me

over to their place for a drink.

Though we've been friends for a while,

as in we've exchanged logins

to a couple streaming apps, I've

never seen the inside of their
 apartment,

but I know they live without
 roommates.

I imagined something reasonable: Ikea,
 maybe

a coffee table, a correlation with trends
 and

aesthetics compounded through

capital's stranglehold on our

pataphysical relation to what

we imagine as signifiers of ourselves.

It was exactly like that. We watched

an episode of *Twin Peaks*

(third season, which I'd already seen),

the one where the goblin in the box

shreds those two teenagers. I was

high and a little freaked out—less due

to Lynch than my own underlying

anticipation of a sporadic, structureless

panic—and walked home that evening,

nibbling my friend's water crackers.

I used to suffer terrible anxiety

attacks, existential terror

sirening through me and parking

in my collar, floodlights shining,

filling in the gaps between my bones.

I still have them, but they are less
   frequent,

their mitigation a remedy of CBT and

on-again, off-again analysis. I think

I need to relax. Should I relax?

Okay, I'm relaxing. I have my friend's

password to his Shudder account.

Zombi 2 (1979) and *Tourist Trap* (1979),

a camp classic double feature.

A shark attacking the living

dead and—up next—shambling

mannequins who telekinetically
   torment

stranded vacationers have a calming
   influence.

Their excesses, both gore and genre,

render its vehicle so replete each
  becomes

an antidote for any lesser dread.

[BROOKLYN, 10/31/18]

Any writing that doesn't move toward love will
crash against a wall or some other hard surface,
like that time the brakes failed on a train entering
Estación Once.
—CECILIA PAVÓN, "A PERFECT DAY"

Ski pronounced

sky could be a variation on love

when you're not looking and a vital
  whisper

extends as if to say there's something
  here

you can depend on. An unbroken wing

or the last bite of dessert is saved for
  you.

I try searching for Cecilia Pavón's
  website

to gather general information about

my new writer crush, which changes

a few times a year even though

I don't consider myself all that

capricious. I find a Tumblr of hers.

It appears unused and dilapidated

like a shitposting termite crawled

into her admin and filled the
    homepage

with 2015 consumer "Top Best" lists.
    "Top Best Waring

Blenders Reviews 2015," "Top Best
    Ironing Boards

Reviews 2015," "Top Best Pedestal Fans
    Reviews 2015,"

et al. Strange truisms escape from these
    untrustworthy

gateways: "Let's face it. The fast-paced
    lifestyle of today

is tiring and stressful." Someone
   speaking to their friends

a table over from me at the coffee shop
   just said, "Ha ha!

All I know is I don't ever want to work
   again." As if

any life that doesn't move toward love
   will crash against

labor. Vehicles escape through fire in
   harrowing uploads

and leave a lasting impression on the
   film industry. Whenever

disaster strikes, our virtual assessment
   shifts toward reality

as a means to invest in what can't be
   forgotten, what we see

when we close our eyes, which is
   different than love, a thing

that dissolves or burns out or is made
    unobtrusive

at a later point in time. It's a shaky
    definition, lo-fi

lexicology. I'm really asking for a
    friend. I spend

my mornings writing these loose
    poems about the many

ways to say the same thing, often
    sensing the instability of this

time, whether I will write in the span
    allotted or pass

the time with free Wi-Fi with purchase
    of coffee (cappuccino)

before I, moving obliquely toward
    love, crash against labor.

A day's unfinished work waits on a
    hard drive or as neon

Post-its. Consistency and regularity
   alienate as

they push these words—*yesterday,
   today, tomorrow*—

as interlocutors of happenstance
   playing themselves

off as near-divine agenda. A passage
   closes

with a silent though furious whisking,
   spiraling

into an impersonation of place.
   Inextricably knotted to

an unseen, alien terminus, a thread is
   strung into a void

that grows darker as it stretches, and
   believing you can distinguish

anything, you imagine where the
   thread is tied, where you are certain

there is an end because of course. What
    else could be keeping

this thread so taut when you're holding
    only one side?

Rain over a vast body of water

makes little to no difference, and the
    conditions

divert relief even farther from where its
    needed.

The coupon for free refills expired, so I
    hold my finger

over the date, a strategic response to
    inevitability

strip mining our last reliable assets

before a clean sweep shuts everything

in an offsite storage unit. A feasible
    utopia

could be born out of decisions and
    moments

like this? I'm seriously asking. I had a
    car

I sold for rent once. Sometimes I see it
    around.

[BROOKLYN, 11/11/18]

Because I finished something, I thought
I could begin again. It's more a strange
    intervention
of personality that settles on an ending than
    anything else.
When I was younger—maybe you, too—the
    immediate
response would have been inadvertently
    offensive
but I've made a point of exceeding my own
    expectations.
Wild Flowers Out of Gas
by Joe Ceravolo:

Corina gave this to me oh like eight years ago.
It was a photocopy, but it was her only copy.
Mac had made it for her? He, I know, is a zealot
for Ceravolo, was once caught holding *The
    Hellgate*,
Joe's then-unpublished long poem, to a copy
    machine.
He may have gotten a page or two of part one,
"Testament," which opens on Joe's 35th year,
    with the
sound of sparrows, computers invading the
    penis and breast

or being cleaned away. It's one or the other.
    Joe's god clears
the system or complicates it, a poem of the holy
    body,
its carnal revisions to divinity, dedicated to
    divinity itself. A friend
tweets their mother has passed away, and the
    mentions
trend. I see them all day but don't reply.

[BROOKLYN, 12/12/18]

The global ambience falters

carrying an unsteady tray of iced lattes.

Later, its aura is photographed drifting south.

I couldn't be more middle of the road

unless I Wikipedia'd "Negative Capability,"

which I did. Some decisions leave us

in the dark, but I've found company

there, waggish and ridiculous in what

is that? At least we are accounted for

and on-task so the meeting can begin.

I try keeping notes, and they become

a nearby pencil and an empty book,

signifiers of what I could be doing.

We contain two things, really.

One of them has nothing to do with us at all.

It's like a bad movie levying its critique

through a grotesque embodiment of what

it's seeking to skewer. Look, popular

cinema has an interest in feminism

insofar as it can be used to sell violence to
    women.

I'll pay to see it but let's be clear I was

an easy mark. A few friends post from outside

a detention facility. The polar sun sets behind

the concrete tower in one image. A crowd has
    gathered

to demonstrate and condemn the state and the

attending warden's sociopathic lack of
    compassion.

The incarcerated suffer in Brooklyn

in the sentinel night. I am two hundred miles

away and only now reading the news.

[UPSTATE, 2/2/19]

Peel an orange

and it's more orange.

Blue is the language

the sky speaks.

The human spirit is quiet and

defeated in strokes both slight and
    broad, but

opposition always finds a surface

to lay its instruments on.

A resigned transition of power

cued in time with dinner.

Later, there's a moment

to enjoy the benefits of our situation,

but who am I really talking about?

A gasp of brightness with the
   realization

there had been someone there all along

dragging their feet and kicking up
   more dust.

Synonyms undress as opposites

then a few letters are peeled back

and there's just more language
   underneath.

An element is seen as fruitful.

Light reforms to sparks

no longer thrumming with nature's
   routine

but data-driven and wanting the
   glimmer

of an answer instead. So, we took on
   more work

than we expected. The hours were
  billable

though embarrassing when I look back
  at it.

I'm month to month wondering if

I'll soon burn out. This group text I'm
  on

wakes me before sunrise. Mere
  curiosity

topples whole empires of thought,

helpless in the waves of consciousness

heaped upon myself. I've come to

find, however, under the morning

is only more morning. Funny

how important a subject becomes

when it's the one possible outcome

pulled out of context. Like, there's an
   ethics

of leaving well enough alone as there is

an ethics of breaching a limit

though it is possible

to overextend one's comprehension

through sheer force of enthusiasm

and miss the point entirely

unable to apprehend the thing itself

until it's out of reach, sent

skyward with the rest of our words

for the common generosity uncovered

before the morning takes its first breath

to say criticism has a natural antipathy

with biography as if a life of the mind
were

a post of unassailable neutrality. It
didn't

say that. It said nothing. Earlier, it was
only morning

then. It would go on to say nothing

and even that was only morning, so it
said,

"Peel an orange, and it's the language
the sky speaks."

[UPSTATE, 2/5/19]

This could be about getting a

plan off the ground for what is

thought of as a new season,

moodboarding circumstantial

climate futures, diffuse

daylight, how it divides, or

the miles traveled to a long-
    awaited

destination, catalogs of

prior longing and how

the spread-out potential
    landscape is imagined to draw

open convictions into

the cause of emptiness,

that waving flag misinterpreted

as surrender, a first page

ready to be turned then

finding without encountering

significance what remains

is left until the last instant—

not even kept, just there after all,

and significant as in

someone to talk to.

At the Walt Disney Concert Hall,

The Rite of Spring is piped

through an unpresuming flaw

in an otherwise certain structure

so the public can enjoy

a performance without seeing

the sequestered musicians

adjacent in the auditorium,

hostage to their paying gentry

and their love of beauty,

of realizing it as one would

fill a cup quickly to the brim

then drop by drop

entice an impossible dome

above its edge

no force however

compelling could conscript.

I delete a few images from my
   profile

while waiting for a drink order.

It's a mistake but not really.

I could call an 800 number

or chat a representative for help

like I'd broken my foot

and text, "Help! I've broken

my foot." A placid, bedside

voice personified in neutral

sans-serif would calmly

instruct me on next steps

which in this case would be ironic.

My foot is in fact fine and

what was previously

prescient or imminently knowable

has come to pass, revealed

behind an irresolute partition

or a patio wall, climbing

flowers tucking back

into their pods and vines,

sealed along pink and white

seams and pleats,

futurism usurped

as ideology, our home island

a naval fleet in and of itself

that cannot sink, even when

water unmistakably invades

its gleaming crystal timeshares

and no thought is given

to running away in a pair

of freshly pressed khakis.

There's purpose

in these ineluctable

designs ushered to

implementation, the burst

pipes and collapsing

architectures, masterpieces

fading for decades in an attic

then unfurled and found

crimped and wrinkled, the color

unintended but regretless,

still in motion, operating at

a speed beyond preservation.

[LOS ANGELES, 4/14/19]

If all this new construction

were painted clean as these

hotels in South Beach

maybe the sky would be happier

finding affinity among

its occupants as the friendlier,

newer earth. Do you remember that

Ernie Gehr film where, via

camera trick and glass elevator,

slender buildings impart a weightless idea

of themselves into the air above

San Francisco's financial district, swelling

like a chest does with a breath and

tilting through the frame at a slow, illusory
curve,

a parallax rising in the immediate foreground?

Laughing with objects as if suddenly

humanized is my unabashed kink,

a show of true earnestness

serving as poultice for the senselessness

of its antithesis' credibility, the wild

abstracted or nature taken for its constituent

pieces as metaphor, bits of the world

overheard in the silent tongue spoken

by waning gardens whose caretakers churn

and replant at their discretion, rarely hearing

nascent sprouts pleading back to them.

The neighboring hotel is hosting

an all-day after-party, and so is ours.

Their 180 bpm drum and bass runs

a jagged angle into our slower 4/4 pop, perfect

for those of us coasting on watermelon-flavored
edible.

No matter the number of times

we move lounge chairs, the clashing

versions of indulgence were inescapable.

Marie and I dive into the pool

and, submerged, buffer the music temporarily.

When she surfaces, her face wet,

a small, brown leaf sticks to her lip.

Later, we take turns doing this.

Is it possible for unrelated intimacies

to circulate in such a way they shuck

their proprietary origins and become

common, developing into

a unique composition that's all their own,

so long as they're received

with unfettered concentration?

Vacation is a mindset for the fatally employed,

all that can be felt out through a point of view

that craves frosé. We take a Lyft

to the Pérez museum in the morning

and catch the Beatriz González retrospective.

I don't know her work, and it is clear to me

I had been missing out on something

extraordinary. The show is announced

with two massive, linen panels that,
  unstretched,

reach from ceiling to floor and depict

a single image, a facsimile of what looks like

a Manet painting—though I could be wrong—

recodified in acrylic. González's work unfolds

along these lines throughout the show, moving

from recontextualizing art, cultural, and pop
  history

through medium and color into more decisive

political criticism until ending with depictions
  of

sobbing mothers, those who lost their children,

siblings, or spouses to cartel violence.
  Significant,

though, is alongside these portraits of grief

she paints herself, nude self-portraits, clenched

in the same throes of despair, her skin shifted

across the palate from the others' beige and

distinguished in a doleful, familiar blue.

[MIAMI, 5/10/19]

I love that song

everyone loves,

Leonard Cohen's "Suzanne."

I too want to be fed

tea and oranges and have

my perfect body touched

by a perfect mind, perfect being

what is only my or your own,

only ours and willing to be shared

until there's nothing remaining.

Then, what are we left with?

A fleeting thought. The failed

resuscitation of a word

I can no longer recall that

occurred to me riding stoned

for a cheeseburger. A butt-dialed

kiss goodnight. A free day

of Wi-Fi poolside at the Standard

with Mashinka, Danny, and Aaron,

smoking Marlboros and co-working.

A video I took of passing palm trees

at night from the back of a convertible,

which felt lame and was also beautiful.

The bus to lunch with Joseph and Tom,

and I eat it riding a scooter home.

Whole grilled fish with Soph

and Natasha, and I'm so high

I order too much beer

then go bowling and space out

when it's my turn to roll a frame.

A performance-thing then

a dance-thing Amber and I attend.

Maya Deren's house in West
    Hollywood

I never visit because I told Corina

I wouldn't go without her.

A Bas Jan Ader show on Fairfax

I go to alone, watch him eat it

riding his bike into a Dutch canal,

then an Ethiopian restaurant

I didn't know is a date hotspot for
    couples

who hand-feed each other, some

enjoying and others wan while I
    sample

a perfect, peppered split lentil

dish with my own perfect fingers.

A walk up the street from where

I'm staying to Trader Joe's and

I pass the parking lot made

famous by Joni Mitchell, the former

site of The Garden of Alla, an "h"

added to the end when the estate

converted to a hotel under new
    ownership,

originally named for Alla Nazimova,

star and auteur of so many lost films,

her sprawling complex of bungalows

home to a burgeoning queer nightlife

she galvanized in the Hollywood '20s.

Breakfast with Elaine and Robert

and the guy who did the motion-
    capture

for Gollum is a couple tables away

not talking with his girlfriend.

The bus west on Santa Monica

takes me to the pier and I buy

a new beach towel with an

image of the sunset and

"California" written Day-Glo.

The bare facts are strange.

An orange

the color of sky

spirited apart

from matter's cool

reality running

parallel to Venice Beach

where the horizon turns

against us.

[LOS ANGELES, 7/31/19]

I am a survivor of my own ignorance

like everyone else. Eager participation

and consequent points of criticism

outline these years, unironic

and with full sincerity. Well...

there was this time, and it was

as insignificant as it was otherwise

to two or three others before you

grew out of it and into a different set

of roles, projects that ended or were

consumed whole with our inflating beliefs

strategically curious in choking their benefactor

only so much as they will still be able to swallow.

Then it was as if a great wind picked up

the constituent pieces as ornaments

and arranged them across the domestic

apparatus in the shape of a smile.

What use is a tree if not something to fall into?

There's a pocket of undisclosed pleasures

aloft and ballooning over roofs and heads.

Or at least I like to think so, no longer waiting

to come up with a more rational explanation for the

deviations of my personality. It's postmodernity that
  has me

wrecked. A smile that could have been

anyone else's fades into itself, a smile

upon a smile, laughter upon laughter,

a stand of forest, distant yesterday,

arrives as sudden as waking, delivered

at the front steps, then dissolves

with every passing day, maybe less

of itself, maybe more, branches or

the wind between them. The price of fire

…sorry, the price of firing a Taser

is $70 a shot. A rainbow breaks through

the window and moves gradually across

my desk until a little after 3PM.

[BROOKLYN, 10/20/19]

To speak gently with you

makes the whole world again

accessible for a moment.

The spine straightens and shoes

settle evenly on the surface

counting back up from zero to ten.

Health's unlifted veil doesn't conceal

what's horrible or loathsome, not amplifying

what's beautiful or even insignificant

to notoriety. We are occasioned with

a clarity more like generosity, like

closeness, like we've hopped to the bottom of

a well to gather water where it's coolest,

directly from the source, only to look

back up what we thought was this deep

perforation in the earth and see we are still

standing in the open and vibrant field

of the world at hand. This is true

recognition, where the thrill of words

is felt when they emerge without

pulling them from within and are offered

from the world to the world. We are left

with a memorial to this thinking space

errant ideas once occupied, the dispassionate

air in which small, cumulative judgments were

made about people and things—you know—like

what I think about you. I remember this summer.

It was more of a feeling than a vision. An ombré
  rope

knotted with a variety of connections. What was

just enough something to be even more

nothing? There's peace in reconciliation,

I hope. I keep hearing that Skeeter Davis song—

it's the only one I know—"The End of the World."

It would be somewhat ominous, another forecast

for our increasingly lubricated suck into finality,

but it's a song of the immediate aftermath

of heartbreak, of lost love and hopelessness,

true tragedy that doesn't change or waver for 2 ½

minutes. There is nothing more perfect

than a song that doesn't change its mind.

Romeo and Juliet are dead when the play begins,

"star-cross'd lovers take their life," and we watch

anyway, knowing no matter what allusions

or other simple delights can be drawn from

this work, the future is transmitted in a crystal of the
   present,

and we are its engaged monitors, disclosing

more of itself to itself. There is no sudden death,

no startling violence to apprehend. Like Fulci's

promise of a lathe through the eye, we see it
   coming.

It's like generosity, like closeness. And however
   struck

one can be in the mirrored room of eternal
   transfigurations,

it's as Reverdy writes, "The same and single voice
   persisting

in my ear."

[BROOKLYN, 11/26/19]

THE
LANGUAGE
THE SKY SPEAKS

Les vagues mouraient en riant
—PIERRE REVERDY, *CE SOUVENIR*

The waves laughed as they died
is how JA understood it,
translating a causal mystery:
The waves were additionally laughing, not that
they died laughing, but death in its unaltering   5
syntax found company while falling irreparably
    behind
the farthest tide. Some things
seem so real you could reach out and touch them
but I don't know what those things are
do you? Reverdy died at seventy   10
in his monastery bed near where he'd spent
the latter part of his life, devout through most of it,
though he is rumored to have let
his faith go near the end. Maybe
when I die there will be someone to say, "Let go,"   15
    or maybe
I'll be there for someone when
they die, and I'll say, "Let go," and maybe
it will be like letting go or one of us will
laugh because it doesn't at all and we
let go whatever there was to let go well prior to   20
boiling off, our spirit or whatever vapor we are
tumbling through the nearest open window

recondensing as an unrelated tear
unfussed from any emotion, peeking out
25 to wet a distant, dry eye before curling
back under the bottom lid. Whenever we arrive
from somewhere else, we surface into a world that
     doesn't know
us, and where we seem strange even to ourselves.
Like a perennial blooming in its season,
30 we can look at it and say it looks just as it did
last year, so much so it could be the same
except there is something perceptible, feeling
changed even if we can't see it. A show is curtained
mid-performance and the lights cut, but the show
35 is still there; however, we may not know what *there*
     is
anymore. Here and there shift between hands,
one receding into the other, here surging
with a quickening fierceness into there and later
finding its way back to where it thought
40 it had begun, discovering the necessary fragments
     of past
refrains to settle into what can be called home
despite the environment shifting somewhat
drastically. The wind comes sweeping down the
     plain
which I sing to myself in the morning
45 every so often, a camp reminiscence, the roll

out of a personalized kitsch that dissolves the
　　granular
parts of everyday routine and draws them back
as the realization of the present takes precedence.
I'm walking the dog, and I'm singing *Oklahoma*.
It's gray outside, 80° in October, the leaves have not　　50
　　turned
toward the radiance of fall and are still green, not
　　verdant
but sickly. I'm midway into a routine of episodic
　　anhedonia
where desire escapes me entirely. I slip without
　　occasion
into binging on sympathetic moments, and my
　　unconscious
asserts itself while the rest of me takes leave.　　55
There are two people on an exterior bench of this
　　café
looking at me. I stop singing and dive into my
　　phone.
I keep favorite poems in my email drafts:
JA's "When the Sun Went Down," those first lines
I've internalized, Baraka's poem to Jonas, a late　　60
　　poem
from Barbara Guest where "...skies / Throng into
　　themselves..."

Corina's "Pro-Magenta" because I hear her voice
    when I read
"…be a love / That does not know / How to know /
Human genre crashed on / The purblind sea…"

65 Kevin's "The Gifts of San Francisco" that I now
    always have on hand since I looked for it
calmly at Kevin's seaside memorial, not leading on
    about my sudden distress, hearing the soft Fire
Island shore lapping behind the silence of those
    gathered—Corina was there
and Ben, Shiv, and Andrew, too—not remembering
    on the spot which of his books it was in (it's *Tony
    Greene Era*), and instead read a poem from *Tweaky
    Village*, Kevin's review

70 of the years since the start of the second endless US
    invasion of Iraq,
which ends with "So I fucked him. // that's how hot
    he is" and thought Kevin probably loved that,
Ceravolo's *The Hellgate*, its disintegration into
    exaltation,
this C.P. Cavafy poem where he lovingly suckles
the blood from his lover's discarded bandage, "the
    blood of love

75 against my lips," a few anti-capitalist necropastorals
    of César Arconada,
who retreated in exile to the USSR and worked as a
    correspondent

and literary translator for a party-affiliated
   periodical, the anarchist
hymns of Lucía Sánchez Saornil, dedicated to the
   women
she loved while in hiding from Franco in Valencia,
Akilah Oliver's "An Arriving Guard of Angels,   80
   Thusly Coming to Greet,"
a reparative spirit welcoming grief's infinite ingress,
San Juan de la Cruz's "Vivo sin vivir en mí," his holy
   synthesis wants
to keep me intact, life without living, death without
   dying,
Mayröcker's "effulgence of hair" with her "chimera
   / in the morning..."
Mary Ferrari, who is not read widely enough—I   85
   found her work in an early
issue of *The World* stacked with other copies on a
   high shelf at The Poetry Project—
her long poem, "Ode to New York," "I lean against
   / the orange railing of the subway
stairs / the first noon of February / suddenly opens
   up / and becomes
a day of oranges," the third part of *Midwinter Day*
   when Bernadette goes
to town, writing, "There's something about America   90
that's unthinkable..." Schuyler sitting at his desk

again, morning of western New York and
 Baudelaire's skull,
the last poems of Stacy Doris, *Fledge*, which I was
 told were finished
while she was in hospice, the ouroboros of Stevens'
 "Auroras of Autumn,"
95 *Cuidad desde la altura*, what we have of Guillermo
 Bedregal García,
the Rimbaud of La Paz, killed walking across the
 street before he turned thirty,
his verse treatise on death and abyss and image,
 "Las imágenes que
se disuelven en el centro de la lluvia / las imágenes
 que escuchaste…"
Dana's *Some Other Deaths of Bas Jan Ader*, empathy's
100 valiant cheek against the cold tile of dysphoria (my
 best
attempt at approximating Dana's lyric), and
Reverdy's "That Memory," the most beautiful poem
to me in any language, which I save
not only for myself. I am often at metaphorical
105 water's edge when I read these, coming back
to the cusp over which I wait
for myself, gliding pink
noise then waking without
convergence. On like a light.
110 Off light, a light. These days are long and detached

so why make mention of them together?

A sudden deletion of consequence
though the notion had just washed over me.
Someone had left the door wide open
and a lingering stagnation was filtered out like a   115
   shriek
into a plush throw. When pressed firmly
enough, contrivance and a conviction of public
   accountability
form a hazy glass through which I'm viewed
waiting as my laptop decides whether it should
freeze, the staggering icon rotating in spurts   120
then resolving to continue its functions.
Nothing is iced over today despite the now winter
   sky
tumbling near overhead. Ideals nevertheless bridge
a sense of requirement into cozy confidence
belittled and thereby just OK.   125
It's a point where intentions are so rounded
with emotion, moved afield, what is said to be
done is a placebo, absent true interaction,
as any aftermath diffuses and divides
quickly under even the most mild of afternoons,   130
days spent in the park becoming who
we are later, vanished into homes or out of sight
before the temperature drops. At Georgetown

Hospital, there is a series of Sam Gilliam paintings
135 in the foyer. Sam—whose work over the decades
has been most notable for the undulations and
    casual
ripples of his de-stretched canvases, their Dopplers
of saturation that turn away and dip back along
the insouciant shapes of their medium in what
    could
140 be pools if they weren't always in flux—was
commissioned to install a permanent body of
    paintings
to greet and occupy visitors and patients alike
in the clinical environment. These specific pieces
    though
do not share the radical, performative action
145 of his more well-known work—whenever I think of
    it, his 1975
installation at the Philadelphia Museum of Art,
    Seahorses, coasts
to the front of my mind, the piece covering nearly
    an entire exterior
wall of the museum, and because it was the
    apotheosis of Sam's work to that point,
which were these giant, draped canvasses, radiating
    full and bright, it feels so
150 emotional and interpretive I can't help seeing them
    as a critique of deflated social

revolutionary-cum-protoneoliberal projects of white
   folks in the '60s, as if an utter emptiness was
the only promise, evident in these slack, immense
   tie-dyes, but I know
that wasn't necessarily Sam's intent, and it's a failure
   of my own
imagination, the actual story of the canvasses
   involving so much more complexity and balance,
a hurricane, Neptune, and the city of Philadelphia,   155
   a discrete fascination with landscape painting,
especially those formerly in the collection at the
   Corcoran, Sam watching the canvasses,
made from authentic sails, billow in the
   exaggerating storm on the night of
their installation, penumbras cast out into the
   twilight then
slapping back against the museum's marble—and
   are instead framed
squares of perfectly hand-torn paper inundated   160
   with single colors,
brown, red, purple, pink, blue, violet, green,
   orange, black, silver, and yellow,
each one so thoroughly and uniquely suffused as
   though the inks from his other
work had been siphoned and drained into these
   distinct and embodied

variations. The monotypes span two walls of the
    large room
165 I would walk along just to arc around
continuously reviewing the squares until it was time
    to leave.
I even posted a video to my IG story, striding
    around the room
and attempting to capture the pieces within the
    span of whatever
max for video length, a duration likely decided
    through a mean of server
170 space and the time of an average person's rapid,
    visual attention.
My fascination with them was part-incidental—
    institutional settings in idea
require a sterile, intelligible design that's easy to
    maintain
or else can degrade and still retain its message
that this is a room ready to accommodate succor as
    easily as misery
175 no matter how faded the linoleum, and the
    paintings'
sheer presence is at once opposed to this
dichotomy and ratifying insofar as they are
resistant to emotional projection and obliging to
    being stared at

without provoking much critical scrutiny from the
   everyday observer—
and part-genuine enthusiasm. When Paul Reed died   180
one of his obituaries said he was the last of the
   Washington Color School,
and, granted, yes, while he was the last of the six
   men involved in
the originary show at the now-defunct Washington
   Gallery of Modern Art,
I'd always thought of the Color School as more
   expansive including Sam
and other Color Field affiliates in the DC area. This   185
   frothy mix
of ignorance and good intentions led me to email
   the obit's
author and suggest he was white-washing the Color
   School's history,
implying by omission the most prominent Black
   artist
associated with the Color School was not, in fact,
   part of it. His reply was swift
and sharply defensive. He had interviewed Sam not   190
   long before, and Sam himself
said he didn't associate with the Color School even
   if textbooks and
art historians lump him in with this regional coterie.
   I retreated

and apologized, dissolved myself in a culpability
    that the insinuation
was never meant to be so candid and I was
    inquiring off-hand.
195 I wouldn't say it was personally humiliating because
    the conversation was
contained to my professional inbox, but the privacy
    of it felt, in a way, elevated.
Not that my mistranslation of the circumstances was
heighted or escalated in terms of an emotional
    response,
but the conversation suggested a weak abstraction,
200 a sudden opening between understandings that
    becomes
insolvent under the strain of moderate, competing
forces. The nature of it folded me into myself
as though I had stepped into my own breach
where I once was. Abstraction has a dual effect
205 of unintended and intended consequence
wherein a vacuum is left or created.
Context rushes to occupy this space
provided as meaning and collapses
into biography and politics. Le Corbusier
210 designed *Maison Dom-Ino* as a framework for later
adornment and modification though the bare
    construction is

considered an abstract, as much prefigure as it is
    figurative.
Contained within the roil of a medium's framing,
this monstrous fiction of possibility without limits.

I turn my phone over   215
face down on the table
my attention toward something else,
the shallow glow of notifications pulsing,
a crystal eddy suffuse with sunlight on a beachfront
    property,
a reminder with every wheel of the littoral waters   220
    then emptying
with the eventual ebb to a deeper reach
where the world darkens, unfocusing
then beautifully dilated as the grasp of human
    memories
finds fewer and fewer sites of purchase until there's,
    with grace,
nothing left but the sound of music we could never   225
    hope to understand.
I believe this is what Rancière calls the "mutism of
    the orchestra"
though he firmly believes it's a distinct possibility
the mere suggestion of this mutism by way of
    writing
as form is the thing itself, but really, we are not

230 as full of promise as we assume we are,
    reduced to a set of stunning diminutions,
    encirclements rarely encountered
    with adequate notice, the media fashioned
    to foreshadow and translate experience rendered
235 ersatz, tribute to a history impossible to portend.
    I suppose object permanence has to apply
    to things in the past, to the past itself, which is more
    a question of ethics than it is a display of
        intelligence,
    and that is for now a boundary that can't be
        transgressed
240 despite whatever force of grief, nostalgia, or
        intellectual
    misunderstanding pulls us to an edge that from afar
    looked like it might have been the foot of a
        potentially beautiful
    and indecipherably expansive space though when
        surveyed up close
    inquiry dissolves this perception into an impassive
        reflection, you, your immediate
245 surroundings and, rewinding up this glassy
        structure, a continuous emulation
    of the current vaulting overhead in seamless elision,
    "form gulping after formlessness." It's an episode of
        recognition—you know—

the one where, dressed for prom, the middle child
   descends
from the set's back staircase and pauses at the
   railing, apprehensive,
and the family in the flat of the living room,   250
   knowing their date has stood them up,
each turn their eyes downward as the middle child
   startles into view
of their own comprehension before rushing back
   up the staircase
and around the assumed bend of the set. The range
   of absences
this situation accommodates—the affectual in both
   the middle child and, empathically, the family
the bodily in the presumed date and in the   255
   withdrawal of the middle child,
and the material in the implied upstairs—produce a
   series of complimentary vacancies
united as an object of opportunity for the episode's
   viewership, void of pointed symbolism
or ingenious cyphers crafted in committee among
   that season's writing team,
i.e., blue is the representation of this character's
   interiority, its openness or
its willingness to mirror another's interiority to the   260
   detriment of the self,

orange fills the role of objects in the world, the
    sameness encountered among them,
our methods of unraveling each one with precisely
    identical instruments and to
a minor existential effect like how one would sense
    a tang of familiarity in seeing
a swirl in both how they might go about this
    objective engagement then look into
265 the spiral of the Guggenheim after climbing to the
    top; however, the only thought I've ever had
up there is why haven't more people thrown
    themselves over
this low barrier where it's so inviting, so public, and
    would optimistically engage
the mind mid-plummet with contemplation beyond
    absurdity to potential meanings and possibilities
for future interpretation of this action? A point
    opens inside a system that had
270 previously pictured itself indifferent to what the
    casual observer,
you or me, might have to imagine outside of this
    signified and situational reality
arranged in front of us, which at a distance is more
    manageable though no less
barbaric as we negotiate something new and
    coherent apart from it.

By all accounts, it should be summer now. The fresh
    showers of spring
have yet to relent though the imposing eye of a   275
    mid-June
thunderstorm is spectating at the curve
of the earth, set somewhere out west in a routine
plain of level, perspicacious grassland that expands
knowingly as far as anyone's belief who could be
    standing
in the middle of that sort of nowhere, a dry sea   280
    breaking
on the line of an occasional electric fence,
    understanding
a darkening sky. Marie and I saved up and took a
    trip to Kyoto.
There, we walked through a bamboo forest
in early afternoon. The attraction, other than the
    enveloping
verticality of the bamboo, is the euphony made   285
    when
the wind knocks the forest together in a fantastic
    cascade
of percussion and chiming. The forest on that day
    was quiet
and without wind, stark and still as if it had been
    recently

released from someone's steady grip and was
    reacclimating
290 to the edges of itself again, reaching without
touching anything, in advance of the re-
    establishment
of an indiscriminate compassion. This utopic vision,
    though,
is short-lived once the broadcast resumes and the
    laugh track
crashes the sound stage with its chattering
    mechanism,
295 the teeth invisible and skittering across the floor
unwinding their miniature engines from the inside
    out.

Is there a love capable of
communicating, moved to separation
from language in situ and reacclimated, as a
    fragmented statue
300 would, impassioned in its resumed silence, its
    unbroken gaze set
toward their being elsewhere other than here? An
    ankle-high brush against
the lip of a plinth, installed for security, I replay
this kid punching his soda can through Paolo
    Porpora's
Flowers on a crowded afternoon in a Taipei museum

in 2015, his resigned tip into the painting and the   305
   following panic.
To alter art, especially if on accident, strikes me
as essentially ekphrastic, and to review this action
on repeat further embeds it in my mind's
   permanent collection
alongside the songs stuck there—"Drops of Jupiter"
   by Train
is torturously paramount—watching the Diet Coke   310
   biff into
Flowers, my own chuckling like a rustle through a
   hedge before
I shuffle into a dry melancholy over this awful turn
   of events
developing this kid's misprizal of himself,
   diminished in relation to
the perceived value of what he irrefutably affected,
   a striking
dissimilarity to the dutiful, empowered guiltless   315
   who enact
real violence on other people. The replays roll
in sequence, buffering, playing in with amusement
then drawing back in sympathy. Most of the
   morning
rush over with, the café has settled into an easy
   motion,
each customer looping to the counter right in time   320

to replace the last. Someone finishes and gives up
    their seat as another needs it.
There's a shift change and the opening barista heads
    for the door, looking at
their phone. I know them a little, and they give me
    free cappuccinos
whenever they're behind the counter. This
    generosity started when
325   they saw I was reading Emma Goldman, and we
    had a bit of a side
discussion, holding up the line behind me. In
    following days, we
talked about the CNT and the Spanish revolution
    of '36 before
the Nationalist patriarchal faction, fueled by
    momentarily displaced
nobility, clergy, and fascist aspirants, their spite,
    wiped
330   these budding idylls from the country with terrible
    instruments of war
never before witnessed, the revelation of a future
waiting in factories for the spark of delivery and the
    impetus
of a conflict so ideology could justify the isolation
    and harnessing of its most sour
universality, the covetous urge for circumstance
    forcibly made apposite. We talked

about this with some sadness, about Goldman   335
    writing of Berkman's suicide
scarcely weeks before the revolution, that if he
    could have seen
the fruits of his theories and lifelong effort, that if he
    knew
his decades of his dreams of equity and self-
    governance were not
dreams imprisoned, perhaps he would have
    remained and felt a moment,
even, of contentment. There's a means of   340
    understanding Spicer
advocated for in his history classes, when he was
a teacher of history. He began with the present,
    with the news
of the day, then proceeded chronologically into the
    past,
connecting the daily front page over a semester's
    course to ancient
Mesopotamia, a method of interstitial discovery   345
    where students
would sense out the correspondences between
    years, decades, and eras,
moving farther and farther back into record
until eventually hitting myth. Spicer himself
    engaged this technique

in his own writing too, the clearest example being,
   in my opinion,
350 *The Holy Grail* wherein he conflates Arthurian
   legend with, among
many things, the life of Marilyn Monroe, whose
   death was onus
for the book in the first place. Like, how he writes
in "The Book of Lancelot," "Love cannot exist
   between people,"
which, while seemingly ahistorical, is a precise
   example
355 of the indelible connection he senses with the past,
not meaning to diminish our personal relationships,
or like how Goldman writes about love's
   possibilities
when disregarding what she refers to as the
   insurance pact of marriage,
but how Spicer is shown in this photo I found
360 searching for "Jack Spicer Poet" on Google
   Images—
I had to specify "poet" because there's apparently
   another Jack Spicer, and he's
a cartoon—in which he, cupping it by the base of
   the neck, kisses
a disembodied marble head of a man. Now I am
   turning
to structural concerns, how we move on and off

these stages of thought behind the grand drape or   365
  when
the scene is pulled back to reveal another scene
  dressed in a different
dimension of artifice, projecting song to the last
  seats of an empty house,
a fulfillment of a love long after someone has left,
  not unrequited
but never recognized until a harmonic overtone
  crescendos
above the interminable rolling of interior notes and   370
  melodies
then it's as if an awareness is pitched from over the
  shoulder
and across decades previous, slung as far as can be
  seen,
adhering a new explanation to a life of feelings that
  were regarded
as already having their meaning. It is a flood, like
  loss,
spreading out convincingly into the shallows of its   375
  periodic
return to substance, water or sand, the beach where
  Spicer admits
his love for Graham and its futility considering the
  unstoppable tide

that could wash up anywhere, to the feet of
    intractable mountains,

the elasticity of debt as it snaps back with a force of
    interest

380 invented as comparable to the urgency of any
    acquisition

though the erosion of equity is apparent and the
    shearing

masses knife into a transubstantiation no inertia
    could

convince to slow, moving ever more steadily
    without friction,

ever more glamorous to the point of forgetting—is
    it winter again?

385 In an apartment of white and blue décor
    reminiscent of an Aegean

township, books fill one whole wall. There are
    windows big enough

in which someone can be situated, but there's
    uncertainty about

the proceedings. A measure of distraction takes us
    away

from the matter at hand. Early accounts of
    plagiarism

390 and the blank measure of a humming air
    conditioner

thicken the atmosphere and make for stiff
   conversation, lacking
a playfulness that was assumed to be the cardinal
   gesture
marking the occasion, and—it's true—impressions
   felt out
through rough character sketches leave an
   incomplete
portrait. There is a moment of disappointment   395
   meted out
when an ungenerous conception of aesthetics and
   its bearing on
sociality is uncovered without prompting, but it's
   fitting
of attending artistic and philosophical interests
there is a need for a uniform openness and trust, a
   certainty
in one thing, if anything, that there is intelligence in   400
   others
comparable or more acute than one's own, that
   there are
notions, ideas, and references, bold cycles of color
and meaning diverging from one's own imitations,
giving away things one never knew they had or
perhaps never did only to be recovered through   405
   another's

curious needs, an individual real unshaped by
   potentiality,
the stretching fantasies of production on a finite
planet where the page we're on dissolves into a
   digital
fog when our free trial runs out, and we're
   prompted for
410 a credit card number in exchange for a discounted
   subscription
deal promising unremitting access to a crucial
   thread
that, if followed, will lead to a clearing of partial
   insights,
a crown shrugging under the horizon briefly
and with the promise to return if given the time
415 though it's more like a threat, and we're picked up
in a near future, fucking friends in driverless Ubers
   on the BQE,
unmindful of any surveillance apparatus because
   what is privacy
in a security state, post the nudes direct to feed
   anyway
because what else is freedom subsumed under
   categorical control,
420 what else is transcendental than furiously
   overloading

servers kept in those taupe warehouses on the
  suburbs'
selfsame edge proliferating daily, building by
  building, each one
unworked by more than a single person who
  monitors the stacks
and rows of unexpressive data, graveyard-shift
  blowing Addarall
off a decommissioned robot's chrome face that   425
swallows human features into a classical average,
an indistinct look that from far away could be
  anybody
imbued with animation that had at one point
  surged
vitally through its body then withdrew with as
  much
expediency at the moment it was taken offline, the   430
  uncanny
valley dammed and flooded, the veil of
  consciousness
pulled away as the rest of the system is overtaken
  with stasis?
I shut down and step outside. The seasons,
  comprising a symbol
of their whole year's routine, have blended. It's a
  compelling

435   sense of being fractured instead of muddled. Shards
of warmth
glint like intermittent jewels, and a hang of ice
draws down columnar from a cloud full of
screaming
weather and blots out the great orange sun, which
even now
peels off in flares, waves of itself rocketing into
space
440   before gravity returns it to the surface, silent to us.

Notes and Acknowledgements

Parts of *An Orange* have been previously published in *Hyperallergic*, *Fence*, *The Brooklyn Rail*, *The Stinging Fly*, *Blush*, *Sink*, and *Newest York*. Many thanks to Wendy Xu, Paul Legault, Rebecca Wolff, Anselm Berrigan, Cal Doyle, Danny Deton, Jon Ruseski, Steven Karl, and Zach Halberg for their editorial insight and enthusiasm for this work. Additional thanks to Pioneer Works and Wonder for making this book a reality, especially Micaela Durand, Gabriel Florenz, Daniel Kent, and Jeesoo Lee. I'm deeply grateful to those who critiqued poems or manuscript drafts, namely San Juan de la Cruz, Shiv Kotecha, Sophia Le Fraga, and Ken Walker. Also, much gratitude goes to my sister, Leah, my parents, and Helene Bertino for their love and support.

A special thanks to Ben Fama, whose guidance, care, and friendship I could not have written *An Orange* without.

And to Marie-Helene Bertino, for the gifts of time and patience, unwavering encouragement, advice, and love, I am forever grateful.

I would be remiss to not recognize how my own mental health is reflected in this work. If you are depressed or despondent, please do not hesitate to call the National Suicide Prevention Hotline, 1-800-273-8255.

"The Language the Sky Speaks" is written in memory of Tommy Sage Hand.